# UNDERSTANDING
## DRUG USE AND ADDICTION

# OPIOID EDUCATION

**FENTANYL: THE WORLD'S DEADLIEST DRUG**

**HEROIN: DEVASTATING OUR COMMUNITIES**

**PAINKILLERS: THE SCOURGE ON SOCIETY**

**ALTERNATIVE TREATMENTS FOR PAIN MANAGEMENT**

**HOW FIRST RESPONDERS AND ER DOCTORS
SAVE LIVES AND EDUCATE**

**TREATMENTS FOR OPIOID ADDICTION**

**UNDERSTANDING DRUG USE AND ADDICTION**

OPIOID EDUCATION

# UNDERSTANDING

## DRUG USE AND ADDICTION

### ERICA MARCHANT

MC

**MASON CREST**

PHILADELPHIA | MIAMI

## MASON CREST

450 Parkway Drive, Suite D, Broomall, Pennsylvania 19008
(866) MCP-BOOK (toll-free) • www.masoncrest.com

Printed and bound in the United States of America.

CPSIA Compliance Information: Batch #OE2019.
For further information, contact Mason Crest at 1-866-MCP-Book.

First printing

ISBN (hardback) 978-1-4222-4386-2
ISBN (series) 978-1-4222-4378-7
ISBN (ebook) 978-1-4222-7433-0

Library of Congress Cataloging-in-Publication Data on file at the Library of Congress

Interior and cover design: Torque Advertising + Design
Interior layout: Tara Raymo, CreativelyTara
Production: Michelle Luke

Publisher's Note: Websites listed in this book were active at the time of publication. The publisher is not responsible for websites that have changed their address or discontinued operation since the date of publication. The publisher reviews and updates the websites each time the book is reprinted.

## QR CODES AND LINKS TO THIRD-PARTY CONTENT

# CONTENTS

## KEY ICONS TO LOOK FOR:

**Words to Understand:** These words with their easy-to-understand definitions will increase the reader's understanding of the text while building vocabulary skills.

**Sidebars:** This boxed material within the main text allows readers to build knowledge, gain insights, explore possibilities, and broaden their perspectives by weaving together additional information to provide realistic and holistic perspectives.

**Educational videos:** Readers can view videos by scanning our QR codes, providing them with additional educational content to supplement the text. Examples include news coverage, moments in history, speeches, iconic sports moments, and much more!

**Text-Dependent Questions:** These questions send the reader back to the text for more careful attention to the evidence presented there.

**Research Projects:** Readers are pointed toward areas of further inquiry connected to each chapter. Suggestions are provided for projects that encourage deeper research and analysis.

**Series Glossary of Key Terms:** This back-of-the-book glossary contains terminology used throughout this series. Words found here increase the reader's ability to read and comprehend higher-level books and articles in this field.

*Drug addiction is a major problem in the United States. According to the 2017 National Survey on Drug Use and Health, almost 20 million Americans over the age of twelve are battling a drug or alcohol addiction.*

# WORDS TO UNDERSTAND

**detoxification**—the process in which a drug addict stops taking drugs for a period of time, allowing the body to naturally eliminate the psychoactive substances. Also known as "detox."

**euphoria**—feeling intense excitement, happiness, or well-being.

**intervention**—when an action is taken to intervene in a situation that is dangerous or unhealthy.

**peer pressure**—influence from others who are the same age, or in the same social circle.

**rehabilitation**—treatment for drug dependence and addiction at a medical center. Also known as "rehab."

**substance use disorder**—clinical diagnosis of drug abuse or addiction, which can be mild to severe. Causes health issues and social and economic problems.

# CHAPTER 1

# DRUG ABUSE AND ADDICTION

Joey B. wakes up every weekday morning to work as a laborer for a plumbing company. He doesn't have any training as a plumber, so he barely makes more than the minimum wage, and he winds up doing the dirty jobs and heavy lifting that skilled plumbers don't want to do. At thirty-four years old, this is the first job that Joey has held on to for longer than a few months. Unfortunately, this is the best job he can find. He doesn't have a college education or any technical school training. He doesn't even have a high school diploma or GED. Since his teen years, Joey has been an addict, and this is the first time he has held a job and earned a regular paycheck.

Joey's battle with drug addiction began when he was in middle school. One day, a friend of his stole some of his mother's opioid pain medicine, a prescription for oxycodone that she had received from her doctor to treat a chronic condition. The boys thought it would be fun to try the pills together, because they had heard that the drugs would make them feel different. They were young and curious about what it meant to "get high."

Unfortunately for Joey, like so many other young adults that try drugs, that first-time use would lead to years of drug abuse and addiction. Joey liked the way that the drugs made him feel, and he soon wanted more. He couldn't help himself. Opioids are a powerful type of drug that actually change the way that a person's brain works. They can cause a physical dependence that is impossible for users to overcome without going through a **rehabilitation** program.

"Addiction is a chronic disease characterized by drug seeking and use that is compulsive, or difficult to control, despite harmful consequences," notes the National Institute on Drug Abuse. "The initial decision to take drugs is voluntary for most people, but repeated drug use can lead to brain changes that challenge an addicted person's self-control and interfere with their ability to resist intense urges to take drugs. These brain changes can be persistent, which is why drug addiction is considered a 'relapsing' disease—people in recovery from drug use disorders are at increased risk for returning to drug use even after years of not taking the drug."

## The Tragedy of Addiction

Joey abused drugs for over twenty years. As he became addicted, he dropped out of high school and spent much of his young life in and out of jail and being hospitalized. His addiction, and his lack of skills, made it hard for him to find a good job. When he did find work, it often didn't last longer than a few months. His drug abuse interfered with his ability to show up to work on time and manage his responsibilities.

*Drug addiction can make it difficult to hold a steady job.*

While on drugs, he could not function like a normal person and was disoriented, slurred his speech, and couldn't walk properly. When he wasn't taking drugs, he was angry and irritable. It seemed like all his mind could focus on was getting another dose of the drugs.

When Joey wasn't working, he would turn to crime to pay for his addiction. He stole money from his friends and family, and broke into strangers' homes to rob them. During one of his illegal burglaries, he was caught and ended up in jail. But even prison did not stop him from abusing drugs.

One day Joey took so many pills, he suffered an overdose. His mother rushed him to the hospital, and the staff was able to save his life. Even that brush with death did not cure Joey of his addiction, and he continued to abuse drugs. Eventually, taking painkillers wasn't enough for Joey. He turned to heroin, a powerful illegal opiate, in order to feel the "high" that his mind and body could not live without.

While addicted to heroin, Joey lost all his friends; many of them moved on to college and careers. His parents kicked him out of their house, and his family stopped talking to him or inviting him to family events and parties. He wound up moving from house to house, crashing on people's couches, or, when he didn't have a place to stay, sleeping on the streets.

Even though he no longer lived with her, Joey's mom worried about him and cried for him every day. She waited for him to call every morning and prayed that he was alive knowing there were deadly consequences to his drug addiction. Heroin accounts for thousands of overdose deaths every year in the United States. She worried constantly that Joey would become one of those statistics.

Luckily, Joey finally got some real help. He moved out of the state and away from the places and people that had fueled

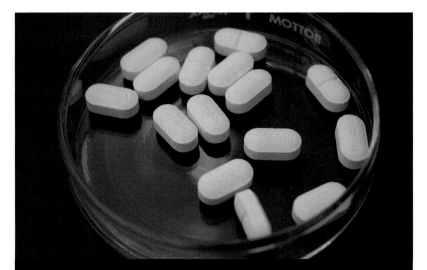

*Some people inaccurately refer to all drugs as narcotics, but only opioids can be properly classified as narcotic drugs. Pictured here is hydrocodone, an opioid pain medication sold under the trade name Vicodin.*

his addiction. First, he checked himself into a **detoxification** center and flushed the drugs from his body. Then, with his mother's financial help, he was able to enroll at a longer-term drug treatment center. It took months of treatment, which cost tens of thousands of dollars, but Joey finally got clean. Today he is trying to amend his life. Joey lives in a home with other sober addicts, attends meetings to stay accountable, and holds a steady job.

Joey's drug addiction caused physical, emotional, and mental damage to himself and his family. He can never get those years back or make up for all the hurt and suffering that came along with his addiction to painkillers and heroin. The physical signs of addiction can never be erased from his body and the hurt and pain his mom suffered for many years will never be forgotten.

Joey's story is just one of millions of addicts across the country. Some started off with prescription drugs, taking them with family or friends and others found drugs on the streets through dealers.

## Understanding Drug Abuse and Addiction

Scientists and researchers have been studying drug abuse and addiction for decades. At one time, drug addiction was seen as a choice, or decision, that people made. From this perspective, getting better and staying sober is also a choice. Many people believed that if a person continued drugs, it was because that person did not want to stop. Thus, addiction often caused others to look down on people like Joey, and people like him were forced to figure things out without any help.

Today, because of scientific advances and discoveries, drug addiction is widely accepted as a medical disorder that has both physical and psychological components. Doctors can monitor

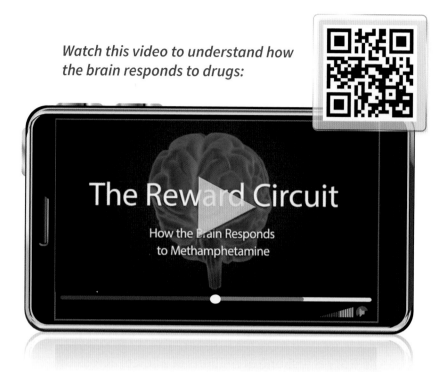

*Watch this video to understand how the brain responds to drugs:*

**The Reward Circuit**

How the Brain Responds to Methamphetamine

addiction in the same way that they would monitor heart disease or another life-threatening health condition. Taking drugs affects the brain and changes a person's behavior. But drug addiction is both preventable and treatable. Doctors and psychologists can treat substance abuse and addiction based on the individual and type of drug being used.

It is important to remember that drugs can be harmful not only to your body and brain but to those who care for and love you. Additionally, when people abuse illegal drugs they expose themselves to serious consequences or addiction. Nevertheless, the annual Monitoring the Future survey conducted by the University of Michigan found in 2018 that 13 percent of eighth graders and 30 percent of tenth graders admitted to trying drugs or alcohol. While that number may seem small—and has grown smaller over the last ten years—it is still alarming.

Addiction acts like any other disease in your body and brain. It changes and disrupts your normal brain and body functions and causes serious and harmful side effects. However, addiction is not only preventable but also treatable. There are programs in place to help people overcome or avoid addiction in the first place, including private and group counseling, rehabilitation clinics, and drug detox centers.

*Clinics like this one in upstate New York provide resources for people recovering from addiction.*

# Why Take Drugs?

There are many reasons why someone might take drugs. Sometimes drugs are prescribed by a doctor or medical professional to relieve pain or other symptoms a person might suffer from. In this case, drug abuse and addiction come from overusing the prescribed medication.

For teens and young adults taking drugs often stems from curiosity and **peer pressure**. Teens tend to participate in more risky behavior than do adults and are more susceptible to

## DANGEROUS DRUGS

Fentanyl is a synthetic opioid, a drug that is manufactured in a laboratory, rather than being produced from the juice of the opium poppy. It is prescribed legally to manage acute and long-term pain, such as that associated with fatal cancers. However, the drug is extremely potent—fifty times stronger than heroin, and 100 times stronger than morphine. Because of this, it has become a popular illegal drug. It is often mixed with heroin, cocaine, or both in order to increase the drug's effect.

As synthetic opioids like fentanyl have become increasingly popular, they have also proven to be increasingly lethal. A buyer of illegal heroin has no way of knowing whether the drug has been laced with fentanyl. This makes it much easier to take too much of the drug, resulting in an overdose. The number of deaths due to fentanyl and other synthetic opioids increased from about 3,000 in 2010 to over 19,400 in 2016. These deaths occurred across all age groups, races, education levels, genders, and regions.

*Opioid painkillers tell the brain to release dopamine and other chemicals that produce good feelings and ease pain.*

peer pressure. Sometimes they are just curious and don't want to disappoint their friends; or they take drugs to impress their friends. Teens may even try illicit substances in order to rebel against parental and legal rules.

Opioids, including heroin, are known to cause **euphoria** and pleasurable feelings, as it changes your brain chemistry. Some people try these drugs simply to find out what it feels like to be high. Others turn to these drugs because they are depressed, stressed out from school, work, or job responsibilities, or because of feeling anxious and overwhelmed. Instead of reaching out for help, they turn to drugs to relax and forget about their problems. However, taking drugs only causes more problems in someone's life.

These drugs appear to produce a positive feeling in a user at first. Users often think they can control their behavior and how often they use the drug or how much they take. With continued use, however, the positive and pleasurable feelings start to go away and the user will need to take more of the drug to maintain what has become a normal feeling to them. Eventually, they will not derive any pleasure and continued drug use is a sign of addiction.

## Abuse versus Addiction

The terms *drug abuse* and *drug addiction* are often used interchangeably, but they can mean different things. Abuse and addiction are connected to each other and drug abuse can lead to addiction if not treated immediately. The truth is, besides being illegal, using or abusing drugs whether only trying them once, using them occasionally, or taking them often is harmful to your brain, your body, and your life.

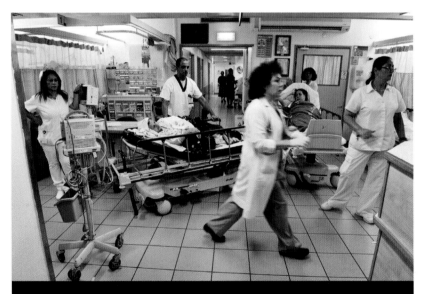

*According to the National Institute on Drug Abuse, addiction costs American society more than $740 billion annually in lost workplace productivity, healthcare expenses, and crime-related costs.*

Drug abuse, or chronic drug use, is considered less damaging than addiction and easier to treat. However, left untreated, drug abuse can lead to a full-blown addiction. Even if a user is not addicted yet, drug abuse carries its own set of problems. Users suffer many consequences related to drug abuse, including legal difficulties, harm to themselves or others, and continued drug use, despite known problems and dangers.

Drug addiction is a chronic disorder characterized by dependence on the drug to function, relapses, and compulsive drug-seeking behavior. The user—the person abusing drugs—suffers physical and psychological withdrawal symptoms when not taking the substance. Addiction is also characterized by increasing use of and need for the illicit drug to achieve the same effects.

Users lose interest in things they once loved including extra-curricular activities, favorite hobbies, and time with family and friends. Everything in their life revolves around using the drug and getting high. Sometimes addicts will deny their own addiction and may or may not attempt to quit. They say things like, "I only use it because I want to," and "I can quit anytime." Such attempts will usually be unsuccessful unless they seek proper medical help and **intervention**.

Someone who is addicted to drugs will continue to use and abuse them despite causing problems that continue to worsen with use. Drug addiction can lead to loss of friends and family and illegal behaviors such as stealing from friends, family, and strangers to get money to pay for drugs, or selling drugs. Those who are addicted are in danger of hurting themselves or others and overdose can lead to brain damage, disability, and even death.

# DRUG OVERDOSE DEATHS IN THE UNITED STATES, 1999-2017

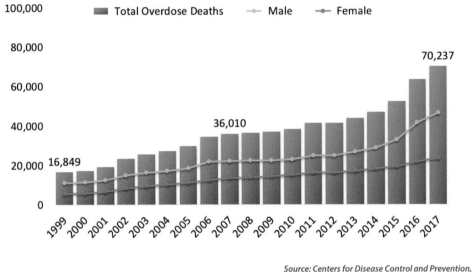

Legend: ■ Total Overdose Deaths —○— Male —●— Female

Y-axis: 100,000 / 80,000 / 60,000 / 40,000 / 20,000 / 0

16,849 · 36,010 · 70,237

X-axis: 1999 2000 2001 2002 2003 2004 2005 2006 2007 2008 2009 2010 2011 2012 2013 2014 2015 2016 2017

Source: Centers for Disease Control and Prevention, National Center for Health Statistics. Released December 2018.

*The rate of drug overdose deaths increased from 6.1 per 100,000 people in 1999 to 21.7 in 2017. The rate rose by 10 percent a year from 1999 through 2006, by 3 percent a year from 2006 through 2014, and by 16 percent a year from 2014 through 2017. Throughout this period, overdose rates were significantly higher for males (rising from 8.2 per 100,000 population in 1999 to 29.1 in 2017) than females (an increase from 3.9 in 1999 to 14.4 in 2017).*

## Substance Use Disorder

Someone who uses drugs or other substances can have a mild to severe case of **substance use disorder**. An individual who receives this clinical diagnosis by a psychiatrist is someone whose regular use of drugs causes impairment ranging from health problems to disability. People who no longer manage their responsibilities effectively, regularly miss school, sports, or work, and stop enjoying things they used to love could be suffering from substance use disorder.

"Addiction is a complex condition, a brain disease that is manifested by compulsive substance use despite harmful consequence," notes the American Psychological Association. "People with addiction (severe substance use disorder) have an intense focus on using a certain substance(s), such as alcohol or drugs, to the point that it takes over their life."

There are different substance use disorders based on the type of addictive drug. For example, Stimulant Use Disorder differs from Hallucinogen Use Disorder, and Opioid Use Disorder differs from both of them. Opioid Use Disorder is

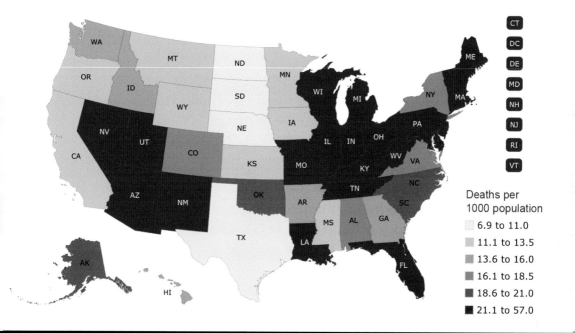

Deaths per
1000 population

6.9 to 11.0
11.1 to 13.5
13.6 to 16.0
16.1 to 18.5
18.6 to 21.0
21.1 to 57.0

*In 2017, 70,237 drug overdose deaths occurred in the United States. Opioids were involved in 68 percent of these cases (47,600 opioid overdose deaths). West Virginia had the highest rate of death due to overdose, followed by Ohio, Pennsylvania, the District of Columbia, and Kentucky. Many states showed statistically significant increases in drug overdose death rates from the previous year.*

diagnosed in someone who abuses or becomes addicted to opioids, a class of drugs that includes certain pain medications as well as illegal drugs like heroin and opium.

Opioids are known to reduce pain. In fact, they are usually prescribed to patients by their doctor after an injury or surgery. However, even when prescribed and monitored by a doctor, opioids are highly addictive, and overusing or abusing a prescription or taking someone else's prescription can lead to Opioid Use Disorder and addiction.

It is important to know that trying these drugs just once can lead to abuse and addiction in anyone. While not everyone becomes addicted, no one is immune to addiction and abuse of opioids and heroin. Taking too much of these drugs, even if prescribed, can cause health problems, decrease a person's breathing, limit oxygen to the brain, and result in coma or death. Taking drugs also affects the people who love and care for the user. It damages relationships and leads to loss in education and opportunity.

While drug use in teens and young adults has decreased in recent years, opioid and heroin-related deaths are occurring at increasing rates. In 2017, over 72,000 Americans died from overdosing on drugs. Almost 50,000 of those people died after overdosing on opioids. Understanding drug abuse and addiction are important to help prevent this crisis in the first place.

1. What are some reasons people use drugs?
2. What does it mean to suffer from substance abuse disorder?
3. What are some of the effects of addiction?

# RESEARCH PROJECT

In 2017, approximately 50,000 people died after overdosing on opioid drugs. But the numbers differ in every state. Use the Internet to find out about the drug death statistics in your state. Write a two-page paper that explains where your state ranks compared to the rest of the United States in the opioid death rate, and what your state is doing to reduce overdose deaths.

*Teenagers often experience mood swings, along with increased feelings of irritability, sadness, and frustration due to the chemical changes that occur as their brains develop. Drug use can intensify these mood swings in young people.*

 WORDS TO UNDERSTAND

**deceit**—to fool people by concealing or hiding the truth.
**neurotransmitters**—chemicals produced in the brain that are used to transmit messages.

# CHAPTER 2

# SYMPTOMS AND SIGNS OF ADDICTION

The symptoms and signs of addiction are subtle at first, but bloom into a greater problem the longer someone uses drugs. Joey, for example, not only thought he had things under control, but his family and friends didn't know he needed help until it was too late. At first, he kept up appearances, but once the addiction took hold, Joey stopped playing sports, constantly skipped school, and began hurting the people that loved and cared for him.

People who abuse drugs can become masters at **deceit**, able to hide their addictions from those who love and care for them. Addiction cannot be treated if the abuser doesn't accept the fact of their addiction. The first step to overcoming addiction and drug abuse is understanding addictive signs and behaviors.

It is important to spot the signs of abuse and addiction early. People who are addicted to drugs will exhibit certain behaviors and characteristics that are different from how they normally act and present themselves. It may be difficult to predict whether drugs are the problem. It is better to talk with a person who might be abusing drugs than to ignore it and watch the person overdose or die from their drug addiction.

It can be particularly hard to spot addiction in teenagers. Their behavior is often unpredictable, and their changing bodies and developing brains can lead to mood swings and behavioral issues that wouldn't normally indicate drug abuse or addiction. How can someone know then, if substance abuse is the problem?

*A sudden lack of interest in sports or activities that a teen was once passionate about could indicate drug use.*

If teens are using drugs and if they've become addicted, they will show other symptoms that may or may not be easily recognizable. People with addiction or substance abuse disorders act in confusing or hurtful ways. They may have mood swings, changes in their behavior, and their actions are uncontrollable or embarrassing.

Unlike smoking and alcohol, opioid and heroin drug use are not accompanied with a smell. Smelling a person's breath or clothes isn't enough to know if he or she is abusing drugs; but there are other ways to tell. Relying on your gut feelings when observing the actions or moods of those suspected of abusing drugs can be helpful, especially if they appear to act differently from how they used to.

## Mood Swings and Behavioral Changes

Being irritable and cranky is almost a rite of passage for teenagers. The ways in which a teenager's body changes during puberty causes it to produce hormones that cause mood swings, sleepiness, and other emotional reactions. When are the mood changes caused by drugs?

Teens who are using drugs may lose motivation to take care of themselves, or stop doing things they used to love. A substance abuser might exhibit unusual signs of anger, hostility, depression, and uneasiness. The user might be unable to keep still or focus on tasks and conversations. Some will lie to parents, or remain secretive about what they are doing, where they are going, or whom they are hanging out with. Others may stop communicating altogether.

Just because a teenager is experiencing wild mood swings doesn't mean he or she is using drugs. But these mood swings can be a signal to parents that they should observe their child more carefully. "Many of the red flags in substance use appear

*During the teen years, clashes with parents are very common. Teens get angry when they feel parents don't respect them or won't give them space to do what they want. Parents get angry because they aren't used to not being in control or they disagree with the teens' decisions.*

in your relationship with the people closest to you," notes the organization Facing Addiction with NCADD. "Having the same fight over and over again, feeling isolated from the people you love, or feeling like you can't reach out for help are all important clues that substance use has become a problem."

Changes in behavior at school are also common with drug use and addiction. These might include youths skipping school when they used to think skipping wasn't okay, or showing up late for school or extracurricular events. Students may stop participating in courses, activities, or sports that they used to love. They may see a drop in their grades, or they may stop doing their homework.

Behavior at home can change as well. The teen drug user may seem jumpy and avoid eye contact when speaking with someone—especially someone in authority. They may act careless or seem clumsy or overtired, as if they haven't slept in days.

Personal relationships can suffer. A teen may stop returning phone calls and text messages. Relationships with family members or friends can change. The teen might dump a best friend, or be unable to coexist with a sibling they were once close with. They can become obnoxious and mean.

Poor hygiene is another potential warning sign of drug abuse. Drug addiction takes control of users' minds, causing them to forget to take care of themselves properly. They may dress messily or wear dirty clothes. They might smell bad from not keeping cleaning or showering, or they may have bad breath. Acne, or other skin issues such as red cheeks, can also be related to drug use. Other physical signs can include needle injection marks (or "track marks") on those who inject heroin, or irritation around the nose for those who snort drugs. Drug abusers often have red eyes or nasal irritation if they crush and snort opioid pills, so if a teen suddenly starts using eye drops or nasal sprays it can be an indication of drug use.

# Recognizing Addiction

Addiction can happen at any age, though studies indicate that it may be more likely if drug use begins when a person is young. "Although taking drugs at any age can lead to addiction, the earlier that drug use begins, the more likely it will progress to addiction," notes the National Institute on Drug Abuse. "This is particularly problematic for teens. Because areas in their brains that control decision-making, judgment, and self-control are still developing, teens may be especially prone to risky behaviors, including trying drugs." It might just take trying a painkiller or heroin one time to become addicted.

It is hard for teens to recognize and accept addictive behavior in themselves. Persons who are addicted will deny their addiction. Deep down they know the addiction or drug abuse is happening, but they may be too embarrassed or disappointed in themselves to admit it. This is why it is harder to realize or admit there may be a problem.

How can teens know if they have an addiction? They will have similar symptoms to those they see in another person who is addicted. Symptoms to look for include unusual changes in attitude and behavior, such as the following:

- Ignoring appearance
- Changing friends or hanging out with different people
- Skipping school or individual classes, and failing to complete school work
- Breaking the law
- Changes in sleeping and eating habits
- Declining interest in favorite activities, such as sports or hobbies

Sometimes, friends and family will approach the teenager to discuss the problem. They might notice a change such as the teen becoming withdrawn or seeming depressed and angry. If drug abuse is the problem, try listening to the teen's concerns. It might mean addiction is the issue and that help is needed right away. If others express concerns it is because they love and care for the person they are concerned about. Drugs destroy lives and can lead to overdose or even death. Family and friends won't want to see that happen to someone they love.

Deep down, a person knows if he or she has an issue with drugs. Asking for help might be difficult, but it is one of the most important things to do to fight and defeat addiction. If speaking with a parent about it is too difficult, try a guidance counselor at school or a medical professional such as a doctor. The sooner the person gets help, the sooner life can get back to normal.

## Physical versus Psychological Addiction

When users are addicted to opioids or heroin and have a substance abuse disorder or become addicted, it means they lose control over their ability to stop using these drugs, even when they want to. Their body or mind craves the drug and cannot function or operate without the drug in their system.

*An opioid drug user who tries to stop taking the drug will experience unpleasant and powerful withdrawal symptoms, including strong cramps and muscle tremors, headaches and dizziness, difficulty breathing, sweating or skin-tingling sensations, and nausea or diarrhea. These occur because the body has become dependent on the drug in order to function properly.*

When a drug users try to stop taking opioids or heroin after becoming addicted they will suffer physical or psychological symptoms and withdrawals.

Addiction changes the brain. Using opioids such as painkillers or heroin causes the brain to release chemicals that affect reward, memory, and motivation systems. Because of this, continued and long-term abuse causes a person to need these drugs to feel normal. At this point, users will feel like they need drugs to survive.

Psychological addiction occurs when there is an emotional or mental craving for a drug. The brain has a strong desire to use the drug and a person who is psychologically addicted will do anything to get the drug of choice, including stealing, lying, and cheating. Mood swings, anxiety, depression, and problems with schoolwork, or losing interest in favorite activities are some signs of psychological addiction.

Physical addiction occurs when the body becomes dependent on opioids or heroin. The body will build up a tolerance to the drug causing the user to need more over time to feel the full effects. When users who are physically addicted to opioids or heroin stop using these drugs, their bodies will suffer extreme withdrawals including sickness, shaking, pain, and other physical symptoms.

Feeling sick or shaky, poor sleeping habits, bad breath, weight loss or gain, and an unkempt appearance are all signs of physical addiction.

A drug abuser can suffer both psychological and physical symptoms of addiction.

## What Are Opioids?

Opioids are a type of drug that imitate **neurotransmitters** by binding themselves to special receptors in the brain, spinal

*To learn how opioids work, scan here:*

cord, and other areas. Chemically, they resemble endorphins, or opioids that our bodies make naturally in order to relieve pain. Opioid drugs are able to reduce feelings of pain by reducing the brain's ability to send pain messages.

The term "opioid" refers to both natural substances and to those drugs that are created from chemicals in laboratories. The natural opioids are also known as opiates. They are derived from the juice of the opium poppy, and include products like opium, morphine, and heroin. Semisynthetic opioids are created in labs when natural opioids are processed with chemicals or blended with other drugs. Some examples include hydromorphone, hydrocodone, and oxycodone. Fully synthetic opioids are completely man-made, but mimic the effects of natural opiates. They include fentanyl, pethidine, levorphanol, methadone, tramadol, and dextropropoxyphene.

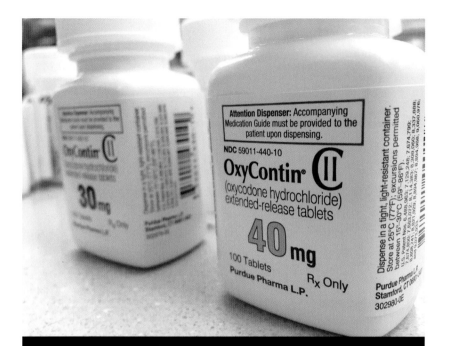

*In recent years, OxyContin manufacturer Purdue Pharma has been targeted with state lawsuits due to the company's deceptive marketing practices. In March 2019 the company settled one case with the state of Oklahoma for $270 million. At that time, hundreds of other lawsuits were still wending their way through the courts.*

Today, many people use the term *opioid* to refer to a class of prescription painkillers. These drugs usually come in pill form, and are only available through a prescription from a doctor. Some of the most common painkillers prescribed today include hydrocodone (sold under the trade name Vicodin), oxycodone (sold as Percocet or OxyContin), codeine, meperidine (sold as Demerol), hydromorphone (sold as Dilaudid), and propoxyphene (sold as Darvon).

In the early twentieth century, heroin was sold as a painkiller, but it was soon taken off the market because of its dangerous side effects. Today, it is a common illegal drug in many cities and communities. Drug cartels from Mexico smuggle large amounts of the drug into the United States, so it is inexpensive and easily available in some areas. Heroin is often sold as a white or brown powder, or as a sticky black tar-like substance that can be injected, smoked, or snorted through the nose.

In recent years, police have found that heroin is often mixed with fentanyl, an extremely powerful opioid. This has led to a spike in the number of drug overdose deaths in the United States.

*Heroin is usually sold as a brown or white powder. White powder heroin has been fully refined, so it is usually the purest and most potent form of the drug. Brown heroin is not as refined, so it is not as potent, but it is usually cheaper because it costs less to produce.*

"Every day, more than 130 people in the United States die after overdosing on opioids," writes the National Institute on Drug Abuse. "The misuse of and addiction to opioids—including prescription pain relievers, heroin, and synthetic opioids such as fentanyl—is a serious national crisis that affects public health as well as social and economic welfare. The Centers for Disease Control and Prevention estimates that the total 'economic burden' of prescription opioid misuse alone in the United States is $78.5 billion a year, including the costs of healthcare, lost productivity, addiction treatment, and criminal justice involvement."

As medical health professionals have become more aware of the scope of the opioid crisis, doctors have cut back on the number of opioid prescriptions. New federal guidelines mean that doctors will often prescribe the drugs only in severe cases, and only for short periods. A person who receives a prescription for opioid painkillers can avoid addiction by carefully following the guidelines about how and when to take the drugs.

1. What are some signs of drug addiction in teens?
2. What is the difference between physical and psychological addiction?
3. What is the difference between prescription opioids and heroin?

 RESEARCH PROJECT

Drugs change the way a person's brain functions. Someone who is addicted to drugs exhibits certain signs and symptoms. Using the Internet, find more information about the risks associated with opioid and heroin addiction, how long it takes to become addicted to different types of drugs, and how long it takes someone to recover from addiction. Research what effect a drug has on a teenager versus an adult. Write the information in a two-page paper, and share it with your class.

*Teens who are bullied in school or have low self-esteem tend to be more likely to try drugs, and therefore more likely to become addicted.*

 WORDS TO UNDERSTAND

**adolescent**—a young person who is developing into an adult; a teenager.

**ethnic**—a population subgroup that shares cultural, linguistic, religious, racial, or national characteristics or traditions.

**self-esteem**—confidence in oneself or one's own worth; self-respect.

# CHAPTER 3

# RISK FACTORS FOR ADDICTION

Addiction does not discriminate. It doesn't care if a person is poor or rich, old or young, what his or her racial, **ethnic**, or religious background is, or if he or she comes from a single-parent household or a large and loving family. Addiction can, and does, happen to anyone.

According to the Center on Addiction, over 40 million people in the United States are addicted to drugs or alcohol. There are more people suffering from addiction than from heart disease, diabetes, or cancer.

Some people believe that addiction is a choice rather than a disease. They think that because an addict chose to start taking drugs, that he or she also can choose to stop using the drugs. It is true that a person exercises a choice the first time he or she decides to try a drug. However, what this doesn't

*Researchers have identified poverty as a major risk factor for drug abuse.*

take into account is that drugs like opioids or heroin changes the user's brain. People who become addicted may no longer have the ability to stop using the drugs, unless they receive outside help.

## Risk Factors for Drug Abuse and Addiction

Addiction does not discriminate based on age, class, status, or any other statistic. Trying a drug just one time can result in abuse and addiction. Addiction can occur at any age, but scientific studies indicate that a person is more likely to become addicted to drugs if he or she begins using them at a young age.

Teens abuse drugs for many reasons, and often these reasons have nothing to do with their home lives. Many former drug addicts have said that they had stable home situations and loving parents. Part of being a teen involves exploring boundaries and taking risks—and taking drugs is a risk. Some **adolescents** try drugs out of boredom or curiosity. Others do so because of peer pressure or a need to ease feelings of pain, sadness, or stress.

Social scientists have identified some risk factors that seem to increase the chance that a teenager will try drugs. Some of these risk factors include the following:

- Poor school performance
- Being bullied or not having any friends
- Feeling worthless and having low **self-esteem**
- Poor relationship with parents or caregivers
- Having family members who abuse drugs or alcohol
- Not understanding the risks associated with drug abuse
- Believing one can control the drug use
- Suffering trauma
- Living in poverty
- Depression, anxiety, or stress

*Young people who are involved with youth organizations like the Boy Scouts tend to be less likely to try drugs.*

On the opposite side of the scale, doctors have identified some factors that decrease the possibility of drug abuse, including the following:

- Having high self-esteem and feelings of worth
- Good friendships and positive role models
- Strong relationships with parents, and a willingness to engage in open-ended discussions about the risks of drug abuse
- Involvement in activities that deter boredom, such as youth organizations and sports
- Understanding the harmful risks associated with drug abuse

## Family History and Genetics

How do family history and genetics play a role in addiction? Teens are more likely to try drugs in the first place and develop drug problems when their parents also abuse drugs.

*To learn more about how people become addicted to drugs, scan here:*

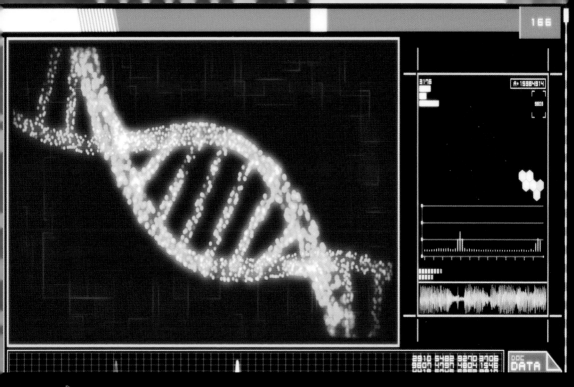

*Heredity plays an important role in addiction. Scientists have found that some people are more likely to become addicted to drugs due to their genetic makeup.*

However, there are plenty of people whose parents are addicts but never try drugs themselves. In fact, the National Institute on Drug Abuse notes that, "most children of parents who abuse alcohol or drugs do not develop alcoholism or addiction themselves."

Genes are units of DNA (deoxyribonucleic acid) that provide the information that directs the body's basic cellular activities. They control a person's physical characteristics, such as height and eye color, but also affect some invisible traits, including the person's susceptibility to problems like heart disease, stroke, diabetes, and addiction. Scientific studies have suggested that genetics may account for about 50 percent of a person's risk of becoming addicted to drugs or alcohol.

Someone whose genes indicate a susceptibility to drug addiction is said to be "genetically predisposed" to addiction. However, just because someone is genetically predisposed doesn't mean that he or she will ever become addicted. The person's environment and experiences also have a strong influence.

"Why do some people become addicted while others don't? Family studies that include identical twins, fraternal twins, adoptees, and siblings suggest that as much as half of a person's risk of becoming addicted to nicotine, alcohol, or other drugs depends on his or her genetic makeup," notes the National Institute on Drug Abuse. "Pinning down the biological basis for this risk is an important avenue of research for scientists trying to solve the problem of drug addiction."

*A mental health condition like depression can be made worse by drug abuse, leading the user into a downward psychological spiral.*

# Depression, Anxiety, and Other Disorders

Having a condition such as clinical depression or anxiety places teens at a higher risk of trying drugs. Teens with psychological disorders might turn to drugs to relieve their symptoms, or to escape from their conditions. They might believe the drugs help them by making bad feelings go away. Unfortunately, this is not the case. Drugs may cause a person to worry less about his or her problems, but those problems do not go away.

This sort of self-medicating happens with both adults and young people. However, since the brains of teenagers are still developing, they are at a much higher risk for becoming addicted.

When drug addiction is the result of a psychiatric condition like depression or bipolar disorder, or occurs in someone who has such a disorder, it creates a situation known as a co-occurring disorder, the diagnostic term used by psychiatrists. Treating both disorders is necessary to successfully break the drug addiction.

# How People Become Addicted

While it might only take one use of drugs to start someone on a path toward addiction, becoming dependent on drugs is not an overnight process. There are many paths one can take toward substance abuse disorders and addiction. Some will use drugs for years before finding they are addicted, and some may use them only a few times before their brain begins to crave the substance and they lose control of their ability to stop using drugs.

Opioids addiction sometimes occurs from overusing a prescription medication prescribed by a doctor. When the doctor stops prescribing the medication, it can lead to seeking alternative ways of finding the drugs or switching from prescription opioids to drugs like heroin or other semisynthetic or man-made drugs.

Sometimes, like in Joey's story in the first chapter, addiction starts with taking a prescription that doesn't belong to you. Teens who have parents or other family members with prescriptions or who use drugs sometimes find ways to steal those drugs for their own use. This is why the family environment can sometimes be a risk factor in teenage drug abuse and addiction. When friends or relatives do drugs around others, they are more likely to try them too.

Anywhere between 25 and 50 percent of those who become addicted suffer long-term effects and relapses after getting sober. This disease, like other diseases, can be prevented by not using drugs. It can also be treated after an addiction occurs through medical intervention, rehabilitation, and programs aimed at helping addicts become sober. Improving health through diet and exercise, saying no to drugs, and influencing others are all ways to fight and prevent addiction.

The longer a teen delays in trying a drug, or not trying it at all, the less likely he or she is to becoming addicted later in life.

## Getting Help for Addiction

It can be hard for teenagers to talk with adults or ask questions about hard subjects like addiction and drug abuse. Teens may find it more comfortable talking with friends their own age than with adults. However, those friends may have many questions that they are not getting answers to either. Without knowing the facts, it can be hard to make decisions.

*Once a person is addicted to a drug like heroin, it is very hard to quit using the drug. Heroin and other opioids change the users body and brain so that they crave the substance, even driving the user to act in self-destructive ways just to get the next dose.*

If it is difficult to speak with parents or ask them questions, going to other trusted sources such as teachers, school counselors, or coaches is another option. A great resource are health teachers or school nurses. They are highly educated in understanding how drugs affect teens. Drug addiction and abuse is a subject considered in many health classes all across America.

When speaking to an adult isn't an option, there are also online resources and help centers that can be contacted. If a friend or loved one has a problem with addiction, it is important to not only talk with that person, but also reach out for help. Later in this book, there is more information about where to get help and how to talk to adults about addiction.

1. What are three risk factors that make a person more likely to become addicted?
2. How does genetics play a role in drug addiction?
3. How many people in America suffer from addiction?

# RESEARCH PROJECT

Using the Internet, search for life stories of addiction in teens. Pick one story and, after doing some research, answer the following questions:

1. Why did this individual begin using drugs?
2. What are some things that might have prevented this individual from becoming addicted?

*The pressure for teenagers to do what others their age are doing can be powerful and hard to resist.*

 WORDS TO UNDERSTAND

**neuroscientist**—someone who studies the nervous system and the ways that the brain, spinal cord, and nerve cells communicate.

**frontal lobe**—the part of the brain located directly behind the forehead and at the front of the brain. It is responsible for learning, behavior, personality, and decision-making.

**prefrontal cortex**—located in the frontal lobe, the prefrontal cortex is the specific part of the brain where decisions are made.

**ventral striatum**—the reward center of the brain.

# CHAPTER 4

# DEALING WITH PEER PRESSURE

Many teens have experienced their parents telling them "no" when asking to do something their friends are doing. Often, their parents follow that "no" up with, "if your friends jumped off a bridge would you also jump off the bridge, too?" It can be hard as a preteen or teen to feel left out. That feeling sometimes leads teenagers to do things they wouldn't otherwise do if their friends weren't doing it too.

Take Joey, for example, as discussed earlier in this book. He started using drugs with his friend. Together they tried drugs and together they became addicted to drugs. While prescription drug abuse and heroin use, on average, have gone down amongst teens—according to a Monitoring the Future study that surveyed over 40,000 students—they are still trying these drugs in significant numbers. Kids try drugs for different reasons, but often peer pressure is the culprit.

*Young people often feel pressure to fit in and be accepted by others. When teens are not sure what to do in a social situation, they often look to others for cues about what is and isn't acceptable.*

In her journals, a young woman named Amy Caruso inadvertently chronicled her fall into drug addiction. The journals began when Amy was in middle school, and ended shortly before Amy's twenty-first birthday, when she died of a heroin overdose. The journals (published as the book *It's Not Gunna Be an Addiction, The Adolescent Journals of Amelia F. W. Caruso*) show how Amy found her self-confidence intertwined in spending time with friends and doing things that she thought would make her look "cool," including drugs. This is how peer pressure works.

# What Is Peer Pressure?

In 80 to 90 percent of cases, adults who abuse or are addicted started taking drugs before the age of 15. That is the age when peer pressure, or influence from kids in the same age group, has the largest hold on the teenage brain. Peer pressure affects everything from social structures and decision-making to the way kids dress and act, and the activities they participate in.

Peer pressure also influences risk-taking behavior in adolescents. When a teen is faced with a situation, such as being offered opioids or heroin they want to reject, they often don't know how to say no. Maybe they are afraid to say no for fear of rejection or losing friends. Peer pressure can be intense for some teens.

A National Institute on Drug Abuse study on peer pressure on adolescents found that teens were more likely to act with

*For tips on avoiding peer pressure, scan here:*

risky behavior when other kids their age, such as their friends, were there to witness it. Risky behavior activates the **ventral striatum**, or reward center, which releases the feel-good chemical dopamine in their brain. The more risks they take, the more dopamine is released. While adults might get a rush from just thinking about taking a risk but not acting on it, teens need to act on the behavior to get the same "feel good" sensations. Merely thinking about it isn't enough. This helps explain why teens are more likely to act on risky behaviors with their friends around than when they are alone. They get a bigger rush of dopamine transmitted through their brain's reward center.

These risky behaviors combined with peer pressure mean teens are more likely to try drugs if their friends are doing it too. Because the teenage brain is still developing, it can be harder to say no when friends or other kids the same age are pressuring a teen to try the drugs too.

According to the National Institute on Drug Abuse, one out of every three pop songs mentions drug use, and three out of every four rap songs include lyrics about drug use.

## Why Teens Are Susceptible to Peer Pressure

The human brain does not stop growing until the mid- to late twenties. Even though the law says a teen is an adult at eighteen, the changing brain isn't quite there yet.

According to **neuroscientist** Dr. Frances Jensen, a professor at the University of Pennsylvania, "the teenage brain is different from the adult brain in several ways," including two important ways that focus around learning and the way brain regions connects to each other.

She says, "the brain is the last organ in the body to mature." Teenagers have more synapses in their brain that are wired for learning than adults. The connection of brain regions begins at the back of the brain and moves to the front. The very last connection the brain makes as it matures is the frontal lobe, at the front of the brain. Why is this important to know? The **frontal lobe** is home to impulse control, judgment, empathy, and decision-making skills. That means teenagers don't access their frontal lobe, or decision-making area of the brain, as fast as an adult does.

"Teenagers are wired to learn faster than adults," and "teen brains are very impressionable." This, Dr. Jensen says, is a good thing and a bad thing. While having these extra synapses is great for learning all the new things that young people will need to know as adults, when it comes to taking drugs their brains are learning a bad thing—addiction.

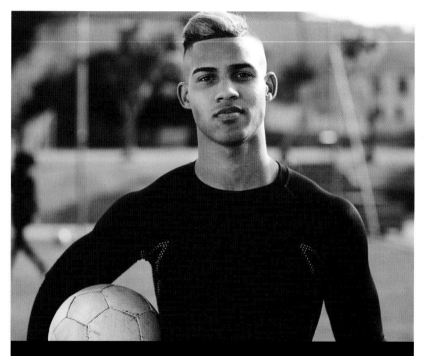

*Self-confident teens are more likely to resist risky suggestions or go along with the crowd. But every young person ends up in a challenging peer pressure situation at some point.*

Combine the way teen brains develop over time with the fact that teens are risk-takers, and this makes addiction easier, faster, and stronger in teens than in adults.

Substances like heroin and other opioids can also change how a teen brain develops and stop the normal process of development before it happens. As a teen takes drugs, the brain is learning to become addicted, to need the drug more, and the drugs are changing the way the brain develops. Not only is it easier for teens to become addicted but it is harder to recover from addiction as an adult.

Other things that affect the teenage brain include stress about school or social situations, feelings of depression, or family problems. Combining all of these issues with drugs, it is easy to see how teens can become addicted.

During the adolescent years, the **prefrontal cortex**, located in the frontal lobe, develops its own decision-making capabilities. It communicates with the reward center, scientifically named the ventral striatum, allowing a teenager to make decisions without the parental guidance they needed as a child. While this is important for teenagers to grow and learn to live in the world around them as adults, it can also cause them to make rash decisions or mistakes when it comes to something like drugs.

Once addicted, only 39 percent of teens are able to stay clean. They may require multiple rounds of rehab to kick their addiction.

## How to Say No to Peer Pressure

It is easier for teens to become addicted to drugs, and peer pressure influences that addiction. So, how can teens protect themselves from peer pressure, and influence other kids to keep them from trying drugs?

*When teens are aware of potential pressure situations, they can plan for them. For example, if a teen wants to attend a party but thinks they might be offered drugs or alcohol there, they can think ahead about how they will turn down the offer.*

Believe it or not, learning to say "no" is not easy for many people, even when they know that saying "yes" will lead them down a destructive and dangerous path. Most people, especially young people, have grown up wanting to please others and make them happy. Saying no to friends takes inner strength and practice!

"But everybody does it," a person who wants a teen to try drugs might say. "Drugs will make you feel good . . . no one will find out . . . this is cool. Don't you want to be cool?" It's a good idea to be prepared for these sorts of statements, and practice ahead of time to know how to respond. For example, when someone claims, "everybody does it!" some responses might include the following: "Plenty of people don't do drugs," "It doesn't feel right for me," or "I just don't want to try it."

When someone says, "Drugs will make you feel good," some responses might be, "I already feel good," or "I would rather play my [favorite sport or video game] to feel good." You might also point out that drugs only make people feel

*Hanging out with people who have similar interests and attitudes toward life can help teens make good decisions. Friends who support each other make it easier to stand up to peer pressure.*

good for a short time; ultimately, drug users often end up feeling worse than they did when they started using the substances.

When someone says, "You would do this drug with me if you are my friend," some responses might include, "I can still be your friend without doing drugs," or "As my friend, you should understand that I don't want to try drugs."

When a drug user claims, "No one will find out," a person trying to avoid peer pressure might answer by saying, "I am not going to chance it, because if my parents found out I would be in big trouble!"

Jen Mason, a counselor who educates teenagers about the dangers of drugs in a community near Boston, Massachusetts, says, "Young people should learn coping skills when stressful situations arise so they do not turn to substances. Addiction ruins a person's life, most of the time forever, as well as it having a big impact on their family and friends."

When teens practice what to say before a stressful situation arises, they will not only know what to say but be able to say it with confidence. By staying strong and always saying no when it comes to drugs, teens can fight the urge to cave in to peer pressure. And the more they do this, the more they can influence others to say no too.

## Influencing Others

Peer pressure works both ways, because teens mimic each other's behavior. When people are strong enough to say no to drugs, others will follow their lead. According to research published in the *Preventative Medicine Journal*, teens sometimes consider trying drugs because they believe it is normal teenage behavior. When they see others who are not trying drugs, that can reset their expectations.

Amy Caruso, whose story was told through her journals, started off using drugs recreationally with her friends. Once she turned to heroin, she started doing it every day and couldn't stop. She thought she could control her abusive behavior, but it turned out that she couldn't. One of Amy's friends, a boy named Lon, wrote her a note when she was about seventeen years old. She mentioned Lon's note in her journal because it made a big impression on her. Lon told Amy that he was glad she had stopped taking drugs, and that she was such a great person when she wasn't on them. He told Amy that she was perfect just he way she was.

It can be a challenge to influence friends to do the right thing. Lon tried doing just that by talking to Amy about getting off drugs, and encouraging her as she tried to get sober. Teens can make a pact with friends either through a handshake or in writing. Deciding together to not do drugs and creating a pact is a good way to stick to a goal of staying away from substances.

## TEXT-DEPENDENT QUESTIONS

1. What is peer pressure and how does it affect teenage behavior?
2. How does a teenage brain differ from an adult brain?
3. What are three positive ways peer pressure can influence friends to avoid drugs?

## RESEARCH PROJECT

Peer pressure can be difficult to deal with, and often teens are unaware of its influence on their lives. Write a personal essay about a time when peer pressure put you in an uncomfortable situation. What happened? How did you handle it, and what did you do to resolve the situation? Were you able to walk away, or did you give in even though you knew it was wrong?

*A loving family environment in which teenagers can talk about their feelings, and where their self-esteem is boosted, makes them more likely to share their questions and concerns about drugs with parents.*

## WORDS TO UNDERSTAND

**condescending**—to act with disdain or express a feeling of superiority over others.

**intimidate**—producing feelings of fear.

**narc**—a slang term for a police officer who investigates drug use. It is often used to refer to a young person who tells on drug users.

# CHAPTER 5

# TALKING TO ADULTS ABOUT DRUGS AND ADDICTION

It can be extremely difficult for a teenager to talk to adults about what is going on in their lives. Whether it's having a crush or having questions about drugs and alcohol, teens often turn to each other rather than trusted adults. Why is this?

Experts say that as a person's brain develops, so does their decision-making capabilities. This means that during the adolescent years, teenagers no longer need constant, close supervision from their parents. Unlike younger children, teenagers don't need their parents to make all their decisions for them. During this time, teenagers also become more involved in things like school, friends, sports, or other activities. They are able to enjoy a whole new world, one in which their parents do not have control. This can be liberating for the teen, but it can also be very difficult for the parents.

*Teens are more likely to communicate with parents if they feel that their concerns will be heard, and not immediately met with an angry lecture.*

Parents love their children and typically want the best from them. They are used to controlling their children's actions and behaviors. As their children become teenagers, with their own unique personalities and traits, parents must learn how to let go, giving their teens a little more freedom and trusting them to make good decisions on their own. However, teens who feel that they are not given enough freedom may clash with their parents over boundaries.

The tension between teens and parents over freedom and boundaries is an important part of the reason that some young people find it hard to talk to their parents about certain issues, including the use of drugs like opioids or heroin. Teens who have developed a substance abuse disorder or addiction often won't tell anyone. They may believe that they don't have a problem, or that they can control and fix the problem on their own without help.

Often, teens may not want to talk about drugs or addiction because they don't want to disappoint their parents. Teens know how parents react when they make mistakes or get a bad grade in school. They might be afraid that even if they are just curious about drugs, bringing up the subject may cause their parents to think that they are taking them. However, it is important for young people to ask questions of the adults they trust. Teens can reassure their parents that they aren't taking drugs (if they aren't), and if the are using drugs, they can ask their parents for help.

## Communication Is the Key

Because parents are used to being in charge of their children, and telling them what to do, they may speak to them in ways that teens feel are **condescending**. Often, parents feel they know better than their teen because they've lived life longer and have more perspective.

*Scan here to learn more about drug use and addiction:*

Parents don't mean to be disrespectful. Often, they don't even realize that they are being condescending. It's just that they believe strongly that they know what is best for their children. However, when teenagers feel their parent is disrespecting them, they will often shut down, refusing to talk with parents about things that are going on in their lives.

One way that teenagers can help their parents feel comfortable providing greater freedom is to openly communicate about the things that they are doing with their friends. This includes talking about drugs and addiction. When that conversation begins, it's important to be honest and open from the start, and to ask— as well as answer— questions.

*Friends are an essential element of a teenager's social development. It can be extremely hard for teens to resist pressure from their friends, or to tell an adult when a friend is trying something that is not healthy for them, such as drugs.*

If a controversial subject like drugs comes up, a parent may initially get upset, or react in a negative or condescending way. Don't end the conversation there. Give your parent a chance to calm down and think about things. If things get heated, it's OK for both teens and parents to step away from the conversation for a while, but once everyone has had time to cool off, return to discussing the situation.

Be prepared to suffer the consequences if you've done something that is against the rules, or against the law, like trying drugs.

## Keeping Secrets

One reason that teenagers give for not wanting to confide in their parents is that they are concerned parents might not keep their secrets. The teenage years are often awkward, and teenagers are easily embarrassed. Parents, of course, are used to discussing their children's activities with friends and family—they've been bragging about and working over them, since they were born!

It is perfectly appropriate for a teenager to ask his or her mother or father to not discuss their private, personal conversations with anyone else. Start the conversation by saying, "I have something I'd like to talk with you about, but I'd appreciate if you could keep it between us."

Teens who know someone who has a problem with drugs may fear sharing that information with their mom or dad because they think they will talk to the other student's parents, or notify the school or other authorities. Teens don't want to violate their friends' confidence or get them into trouble. In their social circles, this can get them labeled as a squealer or a **narc**. However, instead of avoiding the conversation, it is better to help parents understand why the teen is feeling a reluctance to discuss the matter.

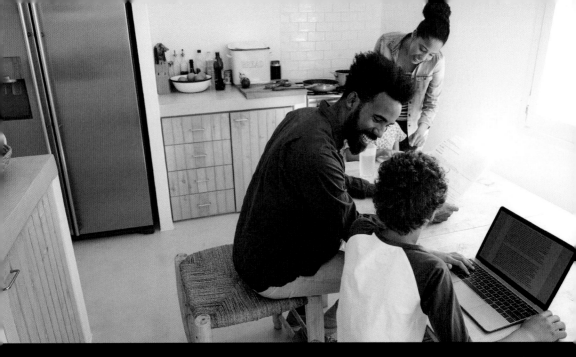

*When parents don't know the answers, they can work with teens to find them online, or arrange to meet with professional counselors who can guide them.*

Teens also have to trust their parents, and recognize that there may be times that they have to reach out to make sure another young person gets help. This is especially true if a friend is abusing drugs or has developed an addiction. It is important to help friends and family, even if it feels like being a tattletale.

## Finding Answers

When it comes to talking about difficult or controversial subjects, parents may be just as uncomfortable talking about things as their teenage children are. In some cases, this is because parents may not know all the answers or the right things to say. Awkwardness might lead a parent to avoid having the discussion, which doesn't help a teenager find the right answers.

If mom or dad don't know the answer, open communication offers a great opportunity to find those answers together. Chances are both parents and teens might have the same questions. There are many great resources available online, including the National Institute on Drug Abuse (www. teens.drugabuse.gov), the Partnership for Drug-Free Kids (www.drugfree.org), or the Center on Addiction (www. centeronaddiction.org).

The National Institute on Drug Abuse is a great resource for teens and parents to learn together about drug addiction from a teenager's point of view. When teens take time to talk with their parents, even if they seem embarrassed or unsure, they will learn to listen and trust more.

# How to Talk to Parents about Drug Abuse and Addiction

Talking to parents about drugs and addiction to substances such as opioids or heroin can be especially difficult— especially if talking about the little stuff doesn't come easy. Even though teens may not need daily guidance and supervision, they do still need their parents' help and support. Teenagers should try to find something to talk to their parents about every day. Even if it's just an update on daily activities, that's fine. The more regularly that teens and parents talk, the easier it will be to communicate when there is a problem.

Before opening up about more difficult subjects such as opioids and heroin addiction think about the end goal of discussing this with parents. It can be hard to start an important conversation, so teens should find a way to get it started. Begin by talking about little things: what was for lunch, a funny thing that happened at school, or something related to a sporting event or activity. Other ideas for conversation starters are a

A risk factor is something that increases your chance of experiencing some event or condition, in this case drug addiction. Just because a person has a risk factor for drug use, that does not mean the person will develop an addiction. It is simply a sign that the person has a greater chance of becoming addicted. Some risk factors for drug addiction include the following:

- A family history of addiction. This could mean that the person inherited a tendency to become addicted to drugs or alcohol.

- Gender. Males are more likely to develop drug problems than females. However, when females become addicts their disease progresses more quickly than in males.

- Having a mental health condition. Depression, Attention Deficit-Hyperactivity Disorder (ADHD), or other conditions make a person more prone to substance abuse.

- Peer pressure. Pressure from friends and other peers to use drugs and alcohols can increase the risk of addiction.

- Family problems. When parents are not involved in a young person's life, if the family is experiencing conflicts, unemployment, or other stressful events, or if teenagers do not receive proper supervision, the risk for substance abuse increases.

- Poverty. Poverty creates difficulties in life that some people try to escape through substance abuse.

favorite sports team, a movie the parent and teen watched together, a good book, or even the neighbor's cat.

Parents love to give advice, but teens hate to take it. Before the important part of the conversation begins, it might be a good idea to ask parents just to listen for now, and not to give advice or try to solve the problem. Reaching out with questions about drugs and addiction is difficult, especially when support is needed.

When the teen is done speaking, the parents may have some thoughts to share—and this will often include their advice on how to handle the situation. If the parent has listened respectfully, then it is up to the teen to listen to what parents are saying as well. The teen may not like or appreciate the

*One of the ways parents meet the needs of their teenagers is by giving them attention. This helps parents and teens to develop closer relationships and builds their confidence and self-esteem.*

parents' advice, or he or she may feel that it isn't helpful, but parents are generally trying to do the right thing and provide help, support, and guidance.

If their teenaged child, or a friend of their child, is in trouble with drugs like opioids or heroin, parents can guide them in the right direction. They may have ideas about where to find help, such as identifying a doctor or a treatment center. They may have good suggestions on how to talk with a friend about their drug abuse.

When reaching out to parents, tweens and teens shouldn't be afraid to tell them the truth. Let them know whether it's just questions borne out of curiosity or if real help is needed. Try not to worry about disappointing them. Simply saying, "I don't want to disappoint you," can often soften the conversation for both kids and parents.

It is okay to feel nervous, embarrassed, or awkward when bringing up a difficult topic like drug addiction. It is possible parents feel the same way. Understanding and overcoming those feelings is a first step in starting a conversation with parents instead of refraining from opening up and asking questions.

Thinking about what to say before the discussion will help make it a clear and concise conversation. Remember to always be honest with them. Always being honest helps parents believe and trust their child. Try to refrain from arguing which can hurt everyone's feelings and cause the conversation to end without getting any results. If an argument brews, take a break from the conversation. Try to relieve the tension with exercise, meditation, art, or another hobby that helps bring calm and focus. Sometimes even crying it out releases the stress and lets kids go back to the conversation with a clear head.

Most importantly, while the conversation shouldn't wait forever, picking the right time for this important discussion

*The National Center on Addiction and Substance Abuse at Columbia University has found that drug abuse in a family increases the likelihood of unhappy marriages and divorce.*

matters. If parents are tired or busy, they are less likely to listen and more likely to react with anger or condescension. One of the best times for tweens and teens to talk with mom or dad is while driving in a car. Having the road or scenery to focus on takes the pressure off both kids and parents while having conversations.

## When the Conversation with Parents Doesn't Happen

There can be many reasons why young adults don't talk with their parents about drugs. Parents usually have their own worries, and their children might be afraid to add to those concerns. Parents might seem busy and unavailable, or in some cases perhaps they are not as supportive of their teenaged children as other parents are. In some cases, parents are divorced, and the teen may feel uncomfortable talking with one parent but not the other.

Sometimes the conversation doesn't occur because mom or dad is the person who is addicted to drugs. The teen may feel **intimidated** or scared to approach his or her parents, or fear that raising the subject will make them angry or defensive. In this scenario, it is important for the teen to remember that a parents' addiction is not a teen's fault. Chapter Six will discuss some general strategies for what to do when a loved one is addicted and where to get help.

If talking with mom or dad isn't an option, teens can turn to another trusted adult. Grandparents, other close relatives, or a family friend may be able to hear concerns and share advice. Other options include a favorite teacher, a trusted coach, a school guidance counselor, or the school nurse.

# TEXT-DEPENDENT QUESTIONS

1. Why is there tension between teenagers and parents over boundaries and freedom?
2. What are two ways in which teens find it difficult to talk to their parents?
3. Whom can teens turn to when they cannot talk with their parents about drugs or addiction?

# RESEARCH PROJECT

For this research project, use the Internet or your school library to find stories about teenagers who became addicted to drugs. Write a two-page report, answering the following questions:

1. Why did this person originally keep his or her drug use from his or her parents?
2. What happened as a result of the continued drug use?
3. In your opinion, what might have changed if this person had spoken with his or her parents or another trusted adult?
4. What would you do if found in the same or a similar situation?

*An intervention is a structured conversation, often facilitated by a specialist, that is intended to show a drug addict how their actions affect their family and friends. The goal of an intervention is to help the addict get into a recovery program.*

##  WORDS TO UNDERSTAND

**behavioral therapy**—a type of therapy often used to treat mental health disorders. The theory is that all behaviors are learned, so unhealthy behaviors can be changed.

**chaos**—complete disorder and confusion.

**incapacitated**—unable to function in a normal way.

# CHAPTER 6

# HELPING A DRUG ADDICT

What should teens do if they think someone they know and care for is addicted to or abusing drugs? It is extremely hard to cope when a loved one has an addiction. Drug abuse and addiction can ruin not only the user's life, but it also hurts those that love and care for the user. Addiction doesn't discriminate—it can happen in any family.

"Dependence on alcohol and drugs is our most serious national public health problem," notes a publication from the US Department of Health and Human Services. "It is prevalent among rich and poor, in all regions of the country, and all ethnic and social groups."

It is scary and stressful living with someone suffering from a substance abuse disorder or addiction. It can cause **chaos** in the home, make kids angry or depressed, and affect many other aspects of their life such as schoolwork and social interactions. In this book you've learned about teens who have suffered addiction, but what if it is your mom or dad or a sibling?

*A medication disposal box in a New York pharmacy allows safe disposal of prescription medicines as a way to prevent drug abuse.*

Oftentimes, your parent doesn't realize how the consequences of his or her drug abuse or addiction affects you. Parents may not have any difficulties holding a job or paying bills, which gives them a false sense that their drug use isn't bad or that they can control it. Sometimes they believe everyone uses drugs as they do. Over time, their drug abuse will likely get worse and cause more problems at home.

It may also be hard to be honest about a loved one having a problem. Admitting the problem is the first step in getting help for that person and for the teen suffering. Getting help for teens of addicted parents is also important. Talk with someone outside of the home such as a counselor, teacher, coach, or a clergy member.

If a family member's addiction is causing an adolescent depression or making them feel that he or she doesn't want to live anymore, that person can contact the National Suicide Prevention Lifeline at 1-800-273-TALK (8255).

*For a short video on why drugs are hard to quit, scan here:*

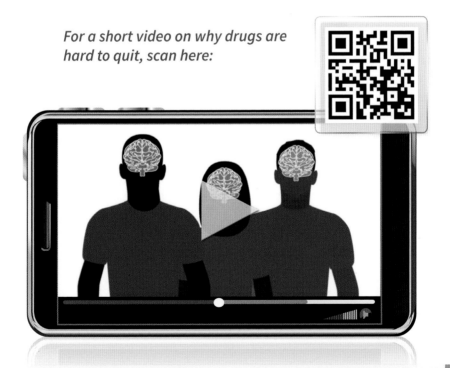

Addicted parents act in confusing and unpredictable ways, break promises, embarrass their kids, and might drive under the influence of drugs. They might even blame their kids for something that isn't their children's fault.

## How to Confront an Addict

If tweens or teens suspect someone they love, like a parent or sibling, is addicted to drugs, the first thing to do is say something. Start by using the steps discussed in chapter five ("Talking to Adults about Addiction") to talk with the parent who is addicted to or abusing drugs. Remember to approach the parent at a time when he or she isn't busy or tired—but also when that parent isn't high on drugs. If the parent always seems to be high on drugs, approaching him or her about it alone might not be the best option.

If talking with parents about their substance abuse isn't an option, try talking with a teacher or another trusted adult who

*It is very hard for drug addicts to admit that they have a problem.*

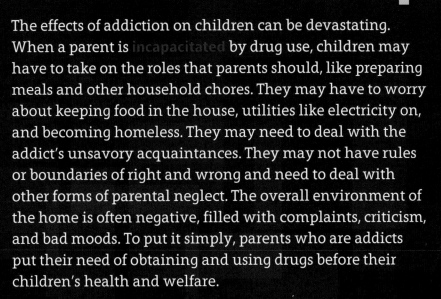

The effects of addiction on children can be devastating. When a parent is incapacitated by drug use, children may have to take on the roles that parents should, like preparing meals and other household chores. They may have to worry about keeping food in the house, utilities like electricity on, and becoming homeless. They may need to deal with the addict's unsavory acquaintances. They may not have rules or boundaries of right and wrong and need to deal with other forms of parental neglect. The overall environment of the home is often negative, filled with complaints, criticism, and bad moods. To put it simply, parents who are addicts put their need of obtaining and using drugs before their children's health and welfare.

Children may be physically or emotionally abused. They may lack proper immunization, medical care, dental treatment, and the basic necessities of food, water, and shelter. Children who grow up in such environments experience long-term difficulties with relationships and may fall into substance abuse themselves or enter into relationships with drug users.

can help confront the parents. Having another supportive adult can give teens the courage needed to broach the subject with a mom or dad.

Many people with substance abuse or addictive disorder will not be able to see their own problems. In this case, talking to someone else about a parent's addiction can be helpful because keeping it bottled up inside can make it harder to deal with.

# Who Should Teens Turn to for Help?

If speaking with a parent alone does not help solve the issue, it is time to go to another trusted family member, a teacher, doctor, or counselor for help. Sometimes, confronting mom or dad might make them angry at first. Tweens and teens should know that they are doing the right thing by bringing attention to the issue and trying to get help. Once parents become sober and get help for their disease, they will realize their children reached out for support because they love their parents.

There are many resources available for teens to get help whether there is or isn't a trusted adult to turn to. The following two resources are especially helpful for teens:

- Alateen, https://al-anon.org/newcomers/teen-corner-alateen/, is a place for teens to go when someone in their family suffers from addiction.
- National Association for Children of Alcoholics, www.nacoa.org

The good news is that anyone can fight addiction to opioids and heroin. Addiction can be treated through rehabilitation, therapy, and recovery. Sometimes this road to recovery starts with an intervention.

# Intervention, Detox, and Rehab

When talking to your parent or sibling alone doesn't persuade them to get help, ask for help from other family members and loved ones. Bringing everyone together to talk with the person suffering from addiction is called an intervention. At an intervention, all members of the family talk about their concerns together and share them with the person suffering from addiction. Everyone should also help the addicted person to understand the current and possible future consequences of continued drug abuse. A professional, such as a therapist or trained specialist, can help your family encourage the person who is addicted to opioids or heroin to seek treatment.

Intervention is sometimes the first step to getting your loved one help. After an intervention, the person might head into a detox program.

At a detox center, those persons who are addicted to drugs will spend time getting the drugs out of their system. For those addicted to opioids, this means that the person will spend days or even weeks suffering from the symptoms of withdrawal. Instead of doing this alone, which can be dangerous and difficult, at a detox center the addict will get rid of the drugs while under the care of a doctor, nurses, and a therapist. There are separate detox programs specifically for teens and adults.

The work isn't over once the drugs are out of their body. After detox, continuing with treatment is important to the recovery of addicts. Many addicts choose to go on to rehab after they detox from opioids and heroin, as this can help them stay sober for the long term.

Rehab, or rehabilitation, is essential to overcome drug addiction. According to the National Institute on Drug Abuse, rehabilitation treatment helps users overcome their addiction by disrupting the effects drugs have on their brain. Rehabilitation can be inpatient or outpatient. The type of rehabilitation depends on the person seeking treatment. A doctor will come up with a comprehensive treatment plan to help your loved one, or you, overcome addiction.

Rehab isn't always the next step after detox, or the final step in the recovery process. Some people diagnosed with a substance abuse disorder or addiction will start with other options or continue on to these options after rehabilitation. They include individual therapy sessions, group therapy with other addicts, **behavioral therapy**, and medical treatment to

*Group therapy, in which addicts discuss their experiences, is often a component of drug rehabilitation programs.*

name a few. Also, seeking treatment for other coexisting disorders such as depression or bipolar disorder is important to maintaining recovery.

One place to find out more about treatment options is the Substance Abuse and Mental Health Services Administration (SAMHSA). This government agency provides confidential help to people seeking treatment for themselves or their loved ones. Their website includes phone numbers for a suicide-prevention helpline, a national helpline for referral treatment, and the Disaster Distress Helpline for those seeking crisis counseling.

If a loved one is addicted to drugs, the most important thing to remember is that his or her addiction is not your fault. Addiction is a disease of the brain, and is not caused by children or young adults.

According to SAMHSA, one in four teens lives in a house dominated by addiction. Addiction and drug abuse affect everyone in the family, so others might need counseling or guidance help also, even though they aren't the one who is addicted. Teens whose relatives suffer from addiction need to know that taking care of themselves and making healthy choices is important. It's a good idea to join a support group or program where you can be honest about your feelings in a supportive environment. Usually, others in these groups are there for the same reasons that you are.

# TEXT-DEPENDENT QUESTIONS

1. What four signs might your parents exhibit if they have a drug addiction?
2. Where can teens turn for help other than from an adult?
3. Name three treatment options to help an abuser or addict stay in recovery.

# RESEARCH PROJECT

According to the National Institute on Drug Abuse (NIDA), a user can successfully manage their addiction, but many addicts will relapse more than once during or after their recovery. This does not mean a treatment doesn't work. Using Internet research, answer the following questions in two to three paragraphs:

1. What are some reasons that drug users relapse during or after their recovery?
2. How can family and friends help someone in recovery stay sober and not abuse drugs again?
3. What other strategies can help addicts continue their treatment and stay in recovery?
4. Why would an abuser or addict need other medications to help with treatment?

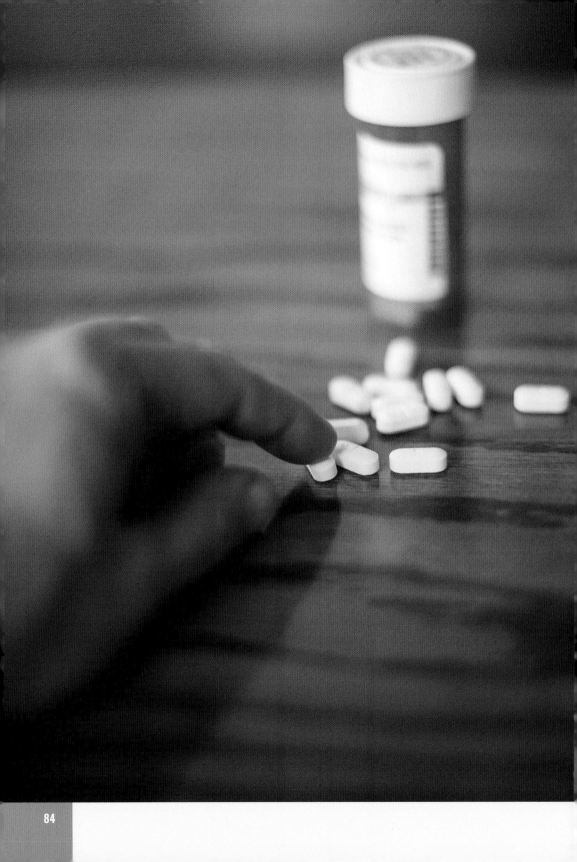

# CHAPTER NOTES

## CHAPTER 1

p. 8: "Addiction is a chronic disease…" National Institute on Drug Abuse, "Understanding Drug Use and Addiction" (accessed May 2019). https://www.drugabuse.gov/publications/drugfacts/understanding-drug-use-addiction

p. 19: "Addiction is a complex condition …" American Psychological Association, "Help With Addiction and Substance Use Disorders" (accessed May 2019). https://www.psychiatry.org/patients-families/addiction

## CHAPTER 2

p. 25: "Many of the red flags …" Facing Addiction with NCADD, "Signs and Symptoms of Addiction" (accessed May 2019). https://www.facingaddiction.org/resources/signs-and-symptoms-of-addiction

p. 27: "Although taking drugs at any age …" National Institute on Drug Abuse, "Understanding Drug Use and Addiction" (accessed May 2019). https://www.drugabuse.gov/publications/drugfacts/understanding-drug-use-addiction

p.34: "Every day, more than 130…" National Institute on Drug Abuse, "Opioid Overdose Crisis," (January 2019). https://www.drugabuse.gov/drugs-abuse/opioids/opioid-overdose-crisis

## CHAPTER 3

p. 41: "most children of parents…" Sara Bellum, "Real Teens Ask: Is Addiction Hereditary?" NIDA for Teens (February 18, 2011). https://teens.drugabuse.gov/blog/post/real-teens-ask-addiction-hereditary

p. 42: "Why do some people become addicted …" National Institute on Drug Abuse, "Genetics and Epigenetics of Addiction" (accessed May 2019). https://www.drugabuse.gov/publications/drugfacts/genetics-epigenetics-addiction

### CHAPTER 4

p. 52:   "The teenage brain is different …" Frances E. Jensen and Amy Ellis Nutt, *The Teenage Brain: A Neuroscientist's Survival Guide to Raising Adolescents and Young Adults* (New York: HarperCollins, 2015).

p. 52:   "The brain is the last organ …" Jensen and Nutt, The Teenage Brain.

p. 53:   "Teenagers are wired …" Jensen and Nutt, *The Teenage Brain*.

p. 53:   "teen brains are very impressionable," Jensen and Nutt, *The Teenage Brain*.

p. 57:   "Young people should learn …" Jen Mason, interview with the author, January 2019).

### CHAPTER 6

p. 75:   "Dependence on alcohol and drugs …" US Department of Health and Human Services, "Alcohol and Drug Addiction Happens in the Best of Families … and it Hurts" (accessed May 2019). https://www.ncadd.org/images/stories/PDF/alcoholanddrugaddictionhappensinthebestoffamilies.pdf

**abstinence**—to refrain from alcohol or drug use.

**analgesic**—any member of a class of drugs used to achieve analgesia, or relief from pain.

**antagonist**—a substance that counteracts the effects of another drug, by interacting with receptors in the brain to prevent drugs from activating the receptor and causing physical or psychological effects.

**cardiovascular system**—the system consisting of the heart and blood vessels. It delivers nutrients and oxygen to all cells in the body.

**central nervous system**—the system consisting of the nerves in the brain and spinal cord. These are greatly affected by opiates and opioids.

**cerebellum**—a part of the brain that helps regulate posture, balance, and coordination. It is also involved in the processes of emotion, motivation, memory, and thought.

**chronic condition**—a medical condition that persists for a long time (at least three months or more).

**craving**—an intense desire for a substance, also called "psychological dependence."

**dependence**—a situation that occurs when opiates or opioids are used so much that the user's body adapts to the drug and only functions normally when the drug is present. When the user attempts to stop using the drug, a physiological reaction known as withdrawal syndrome occurs.

**detoxification**—medical treatment of a drug addict or alcoholic, intended to rid the patient's bloodstream of the psychoactive substance. The addict is usually required to abstain from the drug or alcohol. Also known as "detox," or "managed withdrawal."

**dopamine**—a brain chemical, classified as a neurotransmitter, found in regions of the brain that regulate movement, emotion, motivation, and reinforcement of rewarding behavior. Dopamine release in reward areas of the brain is caused by all drugs to which people can become addicted.

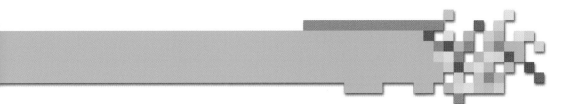

**epidemic**—a widespread occurrence of a disease or illness in a community at a particular time.

**intravenous**—drug delivery through insertion of a needle into a vein.

**intranasal**—drug delivery via inhalation through the nose.

**naloxone**—an antagonist that blocks opioid receptors in the brain, so that they are not activated by opioid drugs. Because it can reverse the problem of opiate intoxication, it is often used to treat overdoses of opioids, such as heroin, fentanyl, or painkillers like oxycodone or hydrocodone.

**neuron**—a unique type of cell found in the brain and throughout the body that specializes in the transmission and processing of information. Also called a "nerve cell."

**opiates**—a drug that is derived directly from the poppy plant, such as opium, heroin, morphine, and codeine.

**opioids**—synthetic drugs that affect the body in a similar way as opiate drugs. The opioids include oxycodone, hydrocodone, fentanyl, and methadone.

**overdose**—the use of any drug in such an amount that serious physical or mental effects occur, including permanent brain damage, coma, or death. The lethal dose of a particular drug can vary depending on the strength of the drug as well as the individual who is taking it.

**relapse**—a return to drug use or drinking after a period of abstinence, often accompanied by a recurrence of drug dependence.

**self-medication**—the use of a drug to lessen the negative effects of stress, anxiety, or other mental disorders without the guidance of a health care provider. Self-medication may lead to addiction and other drug-related problems.

**withdrawal**—a syndrome of often painful physical and psychological symptoms that occurs when someone stops using an addictive drug, such as an opiate or opioid. Often, the drug user will begin taking the drug again to avoid withdrawal.

Gammill, Joani. *Painkillers, Heroin, and the Road to Sanity*. Center City, Minn.: Hazelden, 2014.

Jensen, Frances E., and Amy Ellis Nutt. *The Teenage Brain: A Neuroscientist's Survival Guide to Raising Adolescents and Young Adults*. New York: HarperCollins, 2015.

Parks, Peggy J. *Heroin Addiction*. San Diego, Calif.: ReferencePoint Press, 2015.

Rodriguez, Ray. *Overcoming Prescription Drug Addiction*. Palm Springs, Fla.: Stepping Up Recovery, LLC, 2015.

Sheff, David, and Nic Sheff. *High: Everything You Want to Know About Drugs, Alcohol, and Addiction*. New York: Houghton Mifflin Harcourt Publishing, 2019.

Stolberg, Victor B. *Painkillers: History, Science, and Issues*. Santa Barbara, Calif.: ABC-CLIO, 2016.

Uhl, Xina M. *Preventing and Treating Addiction*. Philadelphia: Mason Crest, 2018.

Melissa M. Weiksnar, ed. *It's Not Gunna Be an Addiction, The Adolescent Journals of Amelia F. W. Caruso (1989-2009)*. Carlisle, Mass.: Amelibro Press, 2014.

*https://teens.drugabuse.gov*
National Institute on Drug Abuse for Teens features drug facts, videos, games, blog posts, and more about staying clean.

*https://www.adolescenthealth.org/Home.aspx*
Society for Adolescent Health and Medicine promotes the health and well-being for adolescents and young adults through advocacy, knowledge, and communication.

*https://www.smartrecovery.org/teens/*
Smart Recovery provides tools and resources to help teens get away from drugs and take back control in their lives.

*https://www.getsmartaboutdrugs.gov/find-help*
Get Smart About Drugs provides a list of resources to help with drug addiction for teens and parents.

*http://www.drugfree.org/stories-of-hope*
Stories of Hope features personal stories of those who have been touched by addiction.

*https://www.drugfreeworld.org/real-life-stories.html*
Foundation for a Drug-Free World International with real life stories of people dealing with drug abuse.

# INDEX

## AUTHOR'S BIOGRAPHY

Erica Marchant is an author, poet, and freelance writer. Her work appears in *The Writers Next Door (2018)* and *On Loss, An Anthology (2019)*. Having grown up with addiction in her family, Erica avoided the struggle herself through education and writing. She now strives to educate others on getting through the teenager years with addicted parents. Erica lives with her husband, three children and two dogs north of Boston, Massachusetts.

## CREDITS

DEA Photo: 10, 33; OTTN Publishing: 18, 19; used under license from Shutterstock, Inc.: 6, 9, 15, 22, 24, 26, 29, 36, 41, 42, 45, 48, 50, 53, 55, 56, 60, 62, 64, 66, 69, 71, 74, 78, 82, 84, 87, 92; ChameleonsEye / Shutterstock.com: 16; Andrew V. Marcus / Shutterstock.com: 38; Pure Radiance Photo / Shutterstock.com: 32; PurpleHousePhotos / Shutterstock.com: 13, 76; Joseph Sohm / Shutterstock.com: 39.